The Tao of Leadership

The Tao of Leadership: Essential Lessons in Wisdom and Purpose

Dr. Scott D. Vinciguerra

The Tao of Leadership
Essential Lessons in Wisdom and Purpose

ISBN – 13:978-1545590775
ISBN – 10:154559077x

Introduction

The following pages offer readers an exploration in connecting the lessons of Lao Tzu's *Tao Te Ching* to contemporary leadership. The book is arranged with a translation of each of Tzu's eighty-one essays, followed by essential lessons for today's leaders regarding the wisdom and purpose of the ancient writing, and how those lessons can be used as a guide for consideration to lead others.

While the Tao is prescriptive, the message for leaders is not. This is a far cry from books that offer a rigid and systematic process for attaining "greatness". While there are many books that offer recommendations to being a 'great' leader, this book simplifies the leader, focusing more on servant leadership, and illuminating the lives of others. Cultivating a rooted system in leading others without oppression, honoring humility in leadership, and attaining greatness as a leader by empowering others are just some of the lessons to be learned. It is my hope that this resource will help you discover your purpose and wisdom, and in that process, illuminate the world around you. Thank you for choosing this text as a partner in that journey.

#1 – The Tao that can be followed is not the eternal Tao.

The name that can be named is not the eternal name.

The nameless is the origin of Heaven and Earth.

While naming is the origin of the myriad things.

Therefore, always desireless, you see the mystery.

Ever desiring, you see the manifestations.

These two are the same – when they appear they are named differently.

The sameness is the mystery,
Mystery within mystery.

The door to all marvels.

➤ Work in leadership to be true to yourself. Don't get caught in the trappings of ego, fame, or false Gods.

➤ Your true purpose rests in your ability to shed the ego for the sake of the task/challenge.

➤ There is an art and science to leading, which is the mystery of watching someone lead. When you look for it, you see it differently than before. You also see the results that stem from your effort and willingness to gaze.

➤ The named and the nameless – the leader and the leading are the mysterious ones. Together woven, opening the opportunity for others to achieve and flourish.

➤ The true leader does not separate himself from the leading. S/he is the one with the task; one with the mission. Part, and parcel.

#2 - All in the world recognize the beautiful as beautiful. Herein lies ugliness.

All recognize the good as good. Herein lies evil.

Therefore, being and non-being produce each other.

Difficulty and ease bring about each other. Long and short delimit each other. High and low rest on each other. Sound and voice harmonize each other. Front and back follow each other.

Therefore, the sage abides in the condition of (Wu-Wei) unattached action. And carries out the wordless teaching. Here, the myriad of things are made, yet not separated.

Therefore, the sage produces without possessing, acts without expectations, and accomplishes without abiding in her accomplishments.

It is precisely because she does not abide in them that they never leave her.

- Your desires to 'make' things happen in leadership is the beginning of your demise. By being mindful of the worthiness you bring to leading, you will focus on the people, not the title.
- Strive to lead holistically through words, silence, action, and inaction. By offering guidance through these principles, leaders rise above the petty, take solace in being reflective, cull away the excess noise of the day, and focus on the true purpose in our soul.
- Once you have identified an agenda, do not allow it to overtake you for the sake of achievement. This desire is brittle, unworthy. Assemble your team to address the root causes of the agenda and the agenda will reveal itself more comprehensively – from here, your path toward solution/resolution will be better spent.
- If leadership is contrived, there are holes in the integrity of every executed decision. By remaining pure, and true to the action of the intention, leading becomes self-sustainable by the people.

#3 – The Tao is so vast that when you use it,
something is always left.

How deep it is!

It seems to be the ancestor of the myriad of things.

It blunts sharpness.

Untangles knots.

Softens the glare.

Unifies with mundane.

It is so full.

It seems to have remainder.

It is the child of I-don't-know-who.

And prior to the primeval Lord-on-high.

- In the midst of leadership, when it becomes an action that is fully taking shape, it is then that the reflective practitioner will begin to see their own way.
- Much like a pebble into water causes ripples, the extension & potential of your leadership has definitive & authentic consequences; yet there is always more that can be done.
- The range of influence through those ripples becomes your offering to others. Nurture it to offer support, so that others may flourish from your insight and selflessness.
- Leadership is complex, yet it can be simple when your purpose is being honored instead of your ego.
- Work to challenge yourself first before you assign responsibility or accountability on others.
- Mingle in the world of those you lead long enough to experience their joy and their pain – their successes and their shortcomings. By appreciating this dynamic through their lens, your vision expands and your soul is righted on a conscious path.

#4 ~ Heaven and Earth are not humane, and regard the people as straw dogs.

The sage is not humane, and regards all things as straw dogs.

The space between Heaven and Earth is just like a bellows; empty it is not exhausted, squeeze it and more comes out.

Investigating it with a lot of talk is not like holding it to the center.

- It is not uncommon for leaders and leadership to feel unjust. That is because of our human frailties. We are an incomplete iteration of our truest, unrealized potential. By being present in this state of agitation and incompleteness, our perspectives become an immediate force in which we focus our thoughts and attention.
- Understanding through wisdom and purpose that all things have a purpose – and once they cease to exist, so too does their purpose. Honoring them (wisdom & purpose) affords the leader to investigate them by contemplating the gifts that they bring to our journey.
- When leaders do not take time to be agitated in their evolution, the bellow remains vacant and the soul unfulfilled. When the bellow is open, breathing a renewed vision of potential, our journey becomes enlightened. Practicing our agitation is the initial phase of development.

#6 – The valley spirit never dies.

It is called, "The Mysterious Female".

The opening of "The Mysterious Female" is called "the root of Heaven and Earth".

Continuous, seeming to remain.

Use it without exertion.

➢ There is a vast current of energy flowing inside many leaders who desire to make a difference in the lives of those they lead. This energy comes intrinsically and is grounded by witnessing the results of the labor.

➢ In this posture, the spirit can never be satisfied – there will always be an unquenchable thirst for more – more progress, more money, more achievement.

➢ Using your "Valley Spirit" wisely will afford you the opportunity to practice discovering the roots of your path.

➢ By remaining centered in your journey, by practicing your commitment to the "Mysterious Female", leaders with conscience will focus their time and energy to a greater good, and not one which can be measured with or by the standard of others; but by a reimagined and renewed "Valley Spirit". Practicing your craft in this way will allow you to exercise your wisdom and purpose naturally, uncontrived and transparent.

#7 – Heaven and Earth last forever.

The reason that Heaven and Earth are able to last forever

Is because they do not give birth to themselves.

Therefore, they are always alive.

Hence, the sage puts herself last and is first.

She is outside herself and therefore her self lasts.

Is it not through her selflessness that she is able to perfect herself?

➤ In the process of seeking your potential as a leader, do so to serve the people, not the ego.

➤ By understanding that only the Heaven and Earth last forever, your position and influence as a leader is temporary. While it may be important to you, to the universe, it represents a grain of sand in all the world's deserts.

➤ As your leadership and purpose evolve they will grow to a place of worthiness. That appreciation comes only to those who are willing to step out of themselves to lead and accept the responsibility to serve.

➤ Leadership and servitude that is sustainable only lasts because it can be sustained on its own; without having to rely on outside forces to uncover its beauty.

#8 – The highest goodness is like water.

Water easily benefits all things without struggle.

Yet, it abides in places that men hate.

Therefore, it is like the Tao.

For dwelling, the Earth is good.

For the mind, depth is good.

The goodness of giving is in the timing.

The goodness of speech is in honesty.

In government, self-mastery is good.

In handling affairs, ability is good.

If you do not wrangle, you will not be blamed.

➢ Do not be the "wrangle" in the lives of those you lead; instead, be the water that provides energy for renewal, and the source of support as a trusted advisor.

➢ Explore and expand your leadership to include areas which are undiscovered or unrealized by your imagination. When parameters are present in your thinking, you will create a small world in which you will be the only one who exists. Dream big without limits to your potential.

➢ Learn to plant your feet firmly on the ground of intuition. Trust the process. In contemplation, seek deeper understanding. Be faithful in your giving to others through a transparent intention. Cultivate a strategy to master yourself first, before laying any judgment on another.

➢ Do not wrangle.

#9 – To hold until full is not as good as stopping.

An over-sharpened sword cannot last long.

A room filled with gold and jewels cannot be protected.

Boasting of your wealth and virtue brings your demise.

After finishing the work, withdraw.

This is the way of Heaven.

➢ Mind every minute of how you spend time leading others. Allow time for growth and expansion in others and yourself. You cannot rush a process that takes time and is developmental. Sit and stop and reflect – otherwise, you will over-lead, and under perform.

➢ As your journey evolves, so too will your rewards. These are inanimate objects, which are only valued to serve a worldly standard.

➢ Do not boast of wealth. In doing so, you sabotage your soul, leaving it vacant of authentic joy.

➢ Do not become a victim of the destination of your journey; however, once the mission is complete, retreat softly to your next Tao.

#10 – Pacifying the agitated material soul and holding
to oneness
Are you able to avoid separation?
Focusing your energy on the release of tension:
Can you be like an infant?

In purifying your insight: can you un-obstruct it?

Loving the people and ruling the state:
Can you avoid over-manipulation?

In opening and closing the gate of Heaven:
Can you be the female?

In illuminating the whole universe:
Can you be free of rationality?

Give birth to it and nourish it.
Produce it, but don't possess it.

Act without expectation.
Excel, but don't take charge.
This is called the "Mysterious Virtue".

➢ In what ways will you allow your intentions and
leadership to be pure? Do you allow the people
to assemble the agenda – to have their voice be
honored? Can your purpose be seen as
manipulation? By seeking truth, the Tao is never
second-guessed.

➢ Wisdom can be discovered in silence. Pure and
utter silence. Free of the bonds of obstruction
and nourished through a selfless soul.
Manifesting your silence, leading an un-
obstructed way, and inviting sustenance will fill
the vacant soul with purpose that is genuine, and
insight that only comes with reflectioned
experience.

➢ Your leadership does not belong to you. It exists
to serve others. By acting without expectation,
by delegating responsibility as needed, the
Mysterious Virtue can be achieved.

#11 – Thirty spokes join together in the hub.

It is because of what is not there that the cart is useful.

Clay is formed into a vessel,
It is because of its emptiness that the vessel is useful.

Cut doors and windows to make a room.
It is because of its emptiness that the room is useful.

Therefore, what is present is used for profit.

But it is in absence that there is usefulness.

➢ The true measures of a highly functioning leader are the actions, which take place without his/her presence. That void, or emptiness allows others to demonstrate their commitment to the purpose. By micromanaging, there is never a void – creativity ceases, collaboration wanes, and compliance is the only rule of day.

➢ A wheel without spokes will eventually crumble on its weight. A vessel will sink without proper balance in buoyancy. A room cannot function to its potential without a window or door to witness the exterior. For each of these to reach their fullest potential, there must be absence to support its intention.

➢ By leading others, to be useful as a leader, there must be moments of absence, which allow others to flourish toward their potential and toward their respective Tao.

#12 – The five colors blind our eyes.

The five tones deafen our ears.

The five flavors confuse our taste.

Racing and hunting madden our minds.

Possessing rare treasures brings about harmful behavior.

Therefore, the sage regards his center, and not his eyes.

He lets go of that, and chooses this.

➤ There will be moments in leadership which tempt you away from your true purpose, and your center. The lure of an attractive opportunity is seductive, clouds your thinking, can temporarily impair your judgment, and bring you further away from your purpose. Wisdom rests in recognizing when these moments present themselves. Racing and hunting for your leadership will only result in emptiness.

➤ By staying true to your center, your path will be fulfilled. Do not chase, hunt, or race. Seek.

#13 – Accept humiliation as a surprise. Value great misfortune as your own self.

What do I mean by "accept humiliation as a surprise?"
When you are humble
Attainment is a surprise.
And so is loss.

That's why I say "accept humiliation as a surprise."

What do I mean by "value great misfortune as your own self?"

If I have no self, how could I experience misfortune?

Therefore, if you dedicate your life for the benefit of the world, you can rely on the world.

If you love dedicating yourself in this way, you can be entrusted with the world.

➤ A leader who is humble seeks understanding, not answers. To let go of yourself is the process by which your servant leadership, wisdom, and purpose will evolve.

➤ In leading others, there is bound to be misfortune along the way. By remaining grounded in understanding that the misfortune is part of your growth process, you will be able to move forward with a resilient spirit.

➤ To be entrusted and rely on the world, the self must be detached from the ego.

#14 – Look for it, it cannot be seen. It is called the distant.
Listen for it, it cannot be heard. It is called the rare.
Reach for it, it cannot be gotten. It is called the subtle.
These three ultimately cannot be fathomed.
Therefore, they join to become one.

Its top is not bright.
Its bottom is not dark; Existing continuously, it cannot be named and it returns to no-thingness.

This is called the formless form.
The image of no-thing.
This is called the most obscure.

Go to meet it, you cannot see its face.
Follow it, you cannot see its back.

By holding to the ancient Tao, you can manage present existence and know the primordial beginning.

This is called the very beginning thread of the Tao.

➢ The leadership journey has many different paths. Your challenge is to discover your own way, or Tao. Your voice, your intentions, your style, are all determined by you. If you aim for perfection, you will always fall short. Strive instead for excellence in your journey.

➢ True leadership has no form – but, the lack of leadership can always be felt, or heard, or seen. The very beginning thread of the Tao is recognizing that the characteristics or attributes of your own leadership do not take form; they only have a presence.

#15 – The ancient masters of the Tao
Had subtle marvelous mystic penetration
A depth that cannot be known.
It is exactly because they are unknowable
that we are forced to pay attention to their appearance.
Hesitant, like one crossing an ice-covered river.
Ready, like one afraid of his neighbors on all sides.
Dignified, like a guest.
Loose, like ice about to melt.
Straightforward, like an un-carved block of wood.
Open, like a valley.
Obscure, like muddy water.

Who can be muddled, and use clarity to gradually become
lucid?
Who can be calm, and use constant application for eventual
success?

The one who holds to this path does not crave fulfillment.
Precisely because he does not crave fulfillment, he can be
shattered
And do without quick restitution.

➤ The enlightened path toward fulfillment is not achieved through a selfish vessel. Craving knowledge, wisdom, or purpose will only lead to an empty destination. Allowing knowledge, wisdom, and purpose to guide you in your Tao is the useful and fulfilling way – by letting in these three gifts, by giving them permission to guide you, your path will become enlightened.

➤ It is through this disposition that clarity can be found. There is no use to micro-managing your path or planning with precise consistency, as you are not fully in control of the future. Because you exist in the now and in the past, does not mean that you can manifest clarity by controlling the future. Learn to be comfortable with the unknown, the unknowing, and the unforeseen, and in doing so, your path will be less agitated with the shortcomings and far more appreciative of the present.

#16 – Effect emptiness to the extreme.
Keep stillness whole.
Myraid of things act in concert.
I therefore watch their return.
All things flourish and each returns to its root.

Returning to the root is called quietude.
Quietude is called returning to life.
Return to life is called constant.
Knowing this constant is called illumination.
Acting arbitrarily without knowing the constant is
harmful.
Knowing the constant is receptivity, which is impartial.

Impartiality is kingship.
Kingship is Heaven.
Heaven is Tao.
Tao is eternal.

Though you lose the body, you do not die.

➤ In your leadership, spend time in quietude. Existing in the moment and stillness of mind, body, and spirit. Exhaust your myriad of things that crowd your mind and your day and allow them to be released from your intention.

➤ In this illumination, your mind will be clear and a renewed sense of your potential will begin to emerge. New ideas, new pathways, new levels of patience with yourself and others, and new layers of appreciation for what exists around you.

➤ By understanding the constant, leaders will not show partiality. Instead, they will see each of the contributions as integral to the success of whole.

#17 – From great antiquity forth they have known and possessed it.
Those of the next level loved and praised it.
The next were in awe of it.
And the next despised it.

If you lack sincerity no one will believe you.

How careful she is with her precious words!
When her work is complete and her job is finished,
Everybody will say, "We did it!"

➢ There is great satisfaction in understanding the process of uniting others toward a common cause. The greatest of leaders embrace a platform of togetherness, and afford each of the members of the team to flourish with their skills sharpened and their confidence installed. To lead in this way empowers others to reach their potential.

➢ However, if the process is met with unclear expectations, ambiguous timelines, or lack of support in words or deeds, the leader sends inconsistent messages and sabotages their own leadership potential. Without complete sincerity, it will be difficult to reach and exceed the standard, which the leader has set forth. Be firm, fair, and consistent – and above all, sincere with your leadership intention.

#18 – When the great Tao perishes
There is humaneness and rightness.

When intelligence is manifest
There is great deception.

When the six relationships are not in harmony
There is filial piety and compassion.

When the country is in chaos
Loyal ministers appear.

➤ Who among your group can be trusted to perform at their fullest potential each and every day? Do you, as the leader, know your people? Are you capable of getting out amongst the people to offer your ear to listen? If the answer is 'yes', then continue to refine these skills. If the answer is 'no', prepare for the house to fall on its own.

➤ In your moments of chaos, who will be your loyal ministers? Will they have the courage to appear and endorse you for your capacity to lead? Will they walk along side you and support you in the best and the worst of times? As a leader, spend time each day teaching others the importance of unity, of teamwork, of achievement for the greater good and not the self. This way, when moments in time become challenging, your team will be prepared and empowered.

#19 – Get rid of "holiness" and abandon "wisdom" and the people will benefit a hundredfold.

Get rid of "humaneness" and abandon "rightness" and the people will return to filial piety and compassion.

Get rid of cleverness and abandon profit, and thieves and gangsters will not exist.

Since the above three are merely words, they are not sufficient.

Therefore there must be something to include them all.

See the origin and keep the non-differentiated state. Lessen selfishness and decrease desire.

➤ Part of the process in discovering who you
   are as a leader offers many choices. By
   choosing to abandon certain practices, you
   will find yourself adopting others.
   Benevolence creates dependence; therefore
   if you seek to develop relationships with
   those you lead, look for ways that you can
   do more with your time and intention, than
   you can with superiority or compliance.

➤ By abandoning all that is worldly in your
   practices, you will be left with the Tao – from
   there, you can dwell the myriad of things.

#20 – Get rid of learning and there will be no anxiety.
How much difference is there between "yes' and "no"?
How far removed from each other are "good" and "evil"?
Yet, what the people are in awe of cannot be disregarded.
I am scattered, never having been in a comfortable center.
All the people enjoy themselves, as if they are at the festival
of the great sacrifice.
Or climbing the Spring Platform.
I alone remain, not yet having shown myself.
Like an infant who has not yet laughed.
Weary, like one despairing of no home to return to.
All the people enjoy extra
While I have left everything behind.
I am ignorant of the minds of others.
So dull!
While average people are clear and bright, I alone am
obscure.
Average people know everything.
To me alone all seems covered.
So flat!
Like the ocean.
Blowing around! It seems there is no place to rest.
Everybody has a goal in mind.
I alone am as ignorant as a bumpkin.
I alone differ from people.
I enjoy being nourished by the mother.

➢ The journey of wisdom and purpose can at times be lonely and unfulfilling. Constantly seeking improvement in all of the areas of your leadership requires a heightened awareness of your strengths, and weaknesses, as well as a concerted effort to nourish that which is in you.

➢ Leading others at certain times can be chaotic, unpredictable, and heavy. However, by finding your 'center', or purpose, you can practice the gift of persistence, diligence, and patience with yourself, and others. Understanding that dynamic is another layer of your development in the journey. From there, experience will offer you wisdom.

➢ Understand that your goals for life-long learning begin and end with your effort. If it is absent from your thought process, it has no home to be nurtured.

#21 – The form of great virtue is something that only the Tao can follow.
The Tao as a "thing" is only vague and obscure.
How obscure! How vague! In it there is form.
How vague! How obscure! In it are things.
How deep! How dark! In it there is an essence.

The essence is so real – therein is belief.

From the present to antiquity, its name has never left it, so we can examine all origins.

How do I know the form of all origins?

By this.

➤ There is great mystery in the Tao that speaks of it being obscure, vague, and elusive. Much like leadership, the gifts you offer others will be unknown to them until they are presented. Getting comfortable with ambiguity as you set out on your journey offers you an opportunity to be at one with the journey. By seeking the essence of your potential as a leader, you can begin to discover a profound sense of peace in your life.

➤ Embrace the ambiguity, challenge the obscure, do a deep-dive into that which seems elusive, and prepare for the unpredictability that comes with leadership. Be open to the endless and powerful possibilities for yourself, and others.

#22 – The imperfect is completed.
The crooked is straight.
The empty is filled.
The old is renewed.
With few there is attainment.
With much there is confusion.
Therefore the sage grasps the one and becomes the model for all.

She does not show herself, and therefore is apparent.
She does not affirm herself, and therefore is acknowledged.
She does not boast and therefore has merit.
She does not strive and is therefore successful.
It is exactly because she does not contend, that nobody can contend with her.

How could the ancient saying, "The imperfect is completed" be regarded as empty talk?

Believe in the complete and return to it.

➤ What messages do you send to others regarding your leadership? Do you seek to show others who is the 'boss'? They likely already know. Do you require affirmation from those you lead in order for your confidence to be re-installed? Do you boast about, claiming and shouting your leadership victories that were achieved on the backs of others? Do you strive for achievements or accolades as the benchmarks of your leadership success? Do you compare and contrast the skills of others and measure that against your own?

➤ By understanding that your imperfections are what you were intended to be made of, do not waste time on perfection, instead, look for the excellence in your life and leadership through the eyes of humility. Only then will your purpose and wisdom be at their highest level of attainment.

#23 – To speak little is natural.
Therefore a gale does not blow a whole morning
Nor does a downpour last a whole day.

Who does these things? Heaven and Earth.
If even Heaven and Earth cannot force perfect
continuity
How can people expect to?

Therefore there is such a thing as aligning one's
actions with the Tao.
If you accord with the Tao you become one with it.
If you accord with virtue, you become one with it.
If you accord with loss you become one with it.

The Tao accepts this accordance gladly.
Virtue accepts this accordance gladly.
Loss also accepts accordance gladly.

If you are untrustworthy, people will not trust you.

➤ Seeking to lead others with perfect continuity is a falsehood that can never exist. Why? Because we are human beings, capable of achieving difficult goals and exceeding them, and equally capable of destroying our lives around us. In leadership, there will be moments where you will be the maestro that modulates the tempo of the symphony; and at other times, it is useful to allow the people to dictate the tempo. Understanding when to use each one depends on your understanding of those you lead, and your willingness to set your ego aside long enough to allow others to thrive.

➤ Knowing that the Tao is capable of teaching you a path, learning can only take place if you are open to receiving it. Because it also accepts and aligns with virtue, loss, pain, and peace, it does not need to offer perfection.

#24 – Standing on tip-toe, you are unsteady.
Straddle-legged, you cannot go.
If you show yourself, you will not be seen.
If you affirm yourself, you will not shine.
If you boast, you will have no merit.
If you promote yourself, you will have no success.

Those who abide in the Tao call these leftover food
and wasted action.
And all things dislike them.

Therefore the person of the Tao does not act like
this.

➢ Be mindful of your words and actions as you lead others. While their eyes are on you, you must reflect a level of sincerity to your disposition and a reverence for your good fortune to lead.

➢ It is not uncommon for leaders to feel a sense of power in the ascension of their careers and leadership responsibilities. However, if you as a leader are willing to trade power for purpose, if you can be courageous enough to set aside self-promotion for the gift of humility, and if you as a leader can shine a light on the people you lead instead of yourself, your Tao will be honored in more satisfying ways than can be measured by worldly standards.

#25 – There is something that is perfect in its disorder
Which is born before Heaven and Earth.
So silent and desolate! It establishes itself without
renewal.
Functions universally without lapse.
We can regard it as the Mother of Everything.

I don't know its name.
Hence, when forced to name it, I call it "Tao".
When forced to categorize it, I call it "great".

Greatness entails transcendence.
Transcendence entails going far.
Going far entails return.
Hence, Tao is great, Heaven is great, the Earth is
great, and the human is also great.
Within our realm there are four greatnesses and the
human being is one of them.

Human beings follow the Earth.
Earth follows heaven.
Heaven follows the Tao
The Tao follows the way things are.

➤ Where does your true greatness rest in your abilities and potential as a leader? Is it in the fashion by which you communicate with others? Is it in organizational skills? Obtaining a clear vision and seeing it to fruition? If the greatness within you is yet to be discovered, consider what it will take in order to achieve that end. Listen to your inner voice that guides your thought process. Seek healthy mentors who can assist to peel away the layers of ambiguity in your journey.

➤ If you are desiring to transform your leadership, the journey must be measured by small achievements. Those achievements could be evidence of many things; how you conduct your meetings, how you organize and prioritize your day, who you decide to align yourself with, and how you see the world around you. From this evidence, you can begin to uncover how these small pieces of a puzzle unite to form a much more complex landscape. Pay attention to the details, be honest with your process, and give 1% more today to others than you did yesterday.

#26 – Heaviness is the root of lightness.
Composure is the rule of instability.
Therefore the sage travels all day
Without putting down his heavy load.
Though there may be spectacles to see
He easily passes them by.

This being so
How could the ruler of a large state
Be so concerned with himself as to ignore the people?

If you take them lightly you will lose your roots.
If you are unstable, you will lose your rulership.

➤ Take a moment to examine what your root system looks like in leadership. Ask yourself if the tree can continue to blossom with what is currently there. Are there elements which weaken your roots? If so, address them, then remove them from your skill-set – they likely aren't helpful today, and likely won't be helpful in the future.

➤ There will always be moments in leadership where it will feel like the heavy load. In those moments, it will challenge your patience, and perhaps your confidence as a leader. In those trying times, go to your people. Ask them for their honesty. Find the low hanging fruit that can be collected that will bring renewal to your day.

#27 – A good traveler leaves no tracks.
Good speech lacks faultfinding.
A good counter needs no calculator.
A well-shut door will stay closed without a latch.
Skillful fastening will stay tied without knots.

It is in this manner that the sage is always skillful in
elevating people.
Therefore she does not discard anybody.

She is always skillful in helping things
Therefore she does not discard anything.
This is called "the actualization of her luminosity".

Hence, the good are the teachers of the not-so-
good.
And the not-so-good are the charges of the good.

Not valuing your teacher or not loving your students:
Even if you are smart, you are gravely in error.

This is called Essential Subtlety.

➤ As leaders, we sometimes forget that we are constantly sending messages to others in our influence. Those messages, good, bad, or indifferent, convey specific ideas to those around us. Much like a teacher has students with a range of abilities and talents, so too do we have individuals who bring a defined skill-set to our workplaces. If our ability to lead is measured by our ability to teach, we must offer a platform for development for each of the people in our charge to evolve.

➤ Remember that you may teach, or lead for 30 years – or your can lead or teach one year, 30 times. The former offers growth and perspective, while the latter uses a cookie-cutter approach to get things done around the office. The former is journey-laden, while the latter is destination driven. The former leaves no tracks, allowing the individual pupil to thrive, while the latter seeks compliance.

#28 – Know the Masculine, cleave to the Feminine
Be the valley for everyone.
Being the valley for everyone
You are always in virtue without lapse.
And you return to infancy.

Know the White, cleave to the Black
Be a model for everyone.
Being the model for everyone
You are always in virtue and free from error
You return to limitlessness.
Know Glory but cleave to Humiliation
Be the valley for everyone.
When your constancy in virtue is complete
You return to the state of the "uncarved block".

The block is cut into implements.
The sage uses them to fulfill roles.

Therefore the great tailor does not cut.

➤ Understanding your role as a leader requires you to know at least two sides of any story which requires the leader to be objective and have a balanced approach to their day. As this disposition is practiced, it becomes refined over time, and returns to a more complete version of your beginning.

➤ Modeling this process for others is a teachable moment in leadership. From this experience, you will demonstrate what you value by how you listen, how your virtues are guided by truth instead of judgment, and how you as the leader expect others within your organization to treat one another.

➤ By being the valley for everyone, you embrace an inclusive environment, and one that is in a constant state of carving the "uncarved block".

#29 – If you want to grab the world and run it
I can see that you will not succeed.
The world is a spiritual vessel, which cannot be
controlled.

Manipulators mess things up.
Grabbers lose it. Therefore:

Sometimes you lead
Sometimes you follow
Sometimes you are stifled
Sometimes you breathe easy
Sometimes you are strong
Sometimes you are weak
Sometimes you destroy
And sometimes you are destroyed

Hence, the sage shuns excess
Shuns grandiosity
Shuns arrogance.

➢ When leaders become a victim of their own success, the house falls. This can happen in very subtle ways – and more than often occurs due to the unraveling of their own leadership. It is common for the seven deadly sins to rear themselves present in leadership: Gluttony, Lust, Greed, Pride, Despondency, Wrath, and Vain – can each play a role in taking down a leader. By being present with your surroundings on a daily basis and keeping your finger on the pulse of your root system, the leader will possess a heightened awareness to warding off these temptations and staying the course for themselves and the people they lead.

➢ Leaders cannot possess that which has no possession. By naming something, or anything, it becomes an entity for possession. Because the world is a spiritual vessel, it cannot be possessed, or controlled.

#30 – If you used the Tao as a principle for ruling
You would not dominate the people by military force.

What goes around comes around.

Where the General has camped
Thorns and bramble grow.
In the wake of a great army
Come years of famine.
If you know what you are doing
You will do what is necessary and stop there.

Accomplish but do not boast
Accomplish without show
Accomplish without arrogance
Accomplish without grabbing
Accomplish without forcing

When things flourish they decline

This is called the non-Tao
The non-Tao is short lived.

➤ In what ways might leaders celebrate their accomplishments? Might they boast about them in social media? Might they seek recognition among their peers? Might they seek to feed their ego through forcing the hands of others in their quest? These too are fleeting elements of a root system incomplete, and a short-sighted mentality for existing *in* the moment instead of *with* the moment.

➤ Being *in* the moment as accomplishments take place is to see yourself as the focal point of the achievement. And while it may be true that your leadership set the course for that to happen, a leader following the Tao steps away, retreating silently. This is what is meant to be *with* the moment. That it becomes a shared experience. That if given the opportunity to look in the mirror, the only reflection would be of the people and their achievements, never those images of the leader themselves.

#31 – Sharp weapons are inauspicious instruments.
Everyone hates them.
Therefore the man of the Tao is not comfortable with them.
In the domestic affairs of the gentleman
The left is the position of honor.
In military affairs the right is the position of honor.

Since weapons are inauspicious instruments, they are not the
instruments of the gentleman
So he uses them without enjoyment
And values plainness.
Victory is never sweet

Those for whom victory is sweet
Are those who enjoy killing.
If you enjoy killing, you cannot gain the trust of the people.

On auspicious occasions the place of honor is on the left
On inauspicious occasions the place of honor is on the right.
The lieutenant commander stands on the left.
The commander-in-chief stands on the right.
And they speak, using funeral rites to bury them.

The common people, from whom all the dead have come to
weep in lamentation.
The victors bury them with funeral rites.

➤ Being involved in leadership means that from time-to-time, you will be involved in a variety of occasions. And in those moments, your weapons will be your words, your actions, your threshold for humility, and your demonstrations of grace. Some of those weapons will be useful to you, others will not. Choose your weapons carefully and strive to understand that victory is not in the battles won or lost, but in the lessons learned along the journey, which anchor the spirit. Examples of victories are not those that stroke the ego, or diminish the person while raising others up, or celebrating good fortune while others suffer. Those are for the ones who "enjoy killing".

➤ If leaders ever desire to see a group of people become immediately unmotivated to perform their important work, violating their trust is the first step to that lonely and desolate journey.

#32 – The Tao is always nameless.
And even though a sapling might be small
No one can make it be his subject.
If rulers could embody this principle
The myriad of things would follow on their own.
Heaven and Earth would be in perfect accord
And rain, sweet dew.

People, unable to deal with It on its own terms
Make adjustments;
And so you have the beginning of division into names.
Since there are already plenty of names
You should know where to stop.
Knowing where to stop, you can avoid danger.

The Tao's existence in the world
Is like valley streams running into the rivers and the
seas.

➢ Moments will come and go in leadership that individuals can reflect upon. Hopefully, for you, many of them will be good. But because we are human beings, we are imperfect. When we accept the Tao as our guiding path, it changes the way we see the world. Tenuous situations no longer become scenarios of winning or losing, rather, they present themselves as moments where we can exercise compromise, or justice, or accountability to ourselves first, before projecting those expectations upon those we lead. Expressing the Tao in our words and deeds helps to teach us when to stop, so that the messages about what we value can be received.

#33 – If you understand others you are smart.
If you understand yourself you are illuminated.
If you overcome others you are powerful.
If you overcome yourself you have strength.
If you know how to be satisfied you are rich.
If you can act with vigor, you have a will.
If you don't lose your objectives you can be long-lasting.

If you die without loss, you are eternal.

➢ One of the lessons of the Tao is to detach the worldly possessions or rewards from the individual. Sacrifice is a daily exercise, and humility and grace become a way of life. These competencies are not often recognized or even honored in leadership, but they are some of the foundational principles of the Tao. If you illuminated your leadership life, what might it look like? Would you rather have power or influence as a tool in your leadership toolbox? Can your will truly know a level of satisfaction in yourself and your spirit? These are the eternal lessons of the Tao.

#34 – The Tao is like a great flooding river. How can it be directed to the left or the right?
The myriad of things rely on it for their life but do not distinguish it.
It brings to completion but cannot be said to exist.

It clothes and feeds all things without lording over them.

It is always desireless, so we call it "the small".
The myriad of things return to it and it doesn't exact lordship.
Thus it can be called "great".
Till the end, it does not regard itself as Great.

Therefore it actualizes its greatness.

➤ Our culture teaches us that leadership should result in 'big' things. Titles, salaries, power, accolades, and greatness become the driving forces for those seeking the path that is burning within to satisfy their leadership appetite. However, in those moments of being 'big', leaders make others feel small. Be mindful of how you make others around you feel as a result of your leadership role.

➤ Excellence in leadership does not lord over others. It's greatness rests in the small and it does not align itself with the greatness that it possesses. It is great because it is small.

#35 – Holding to the Great Form
All pass away.
They pass away unharmed, resting in Great Peace.

It is for food and music that the passing traveler
stops.

When the Tao appears from its opening
It is so subtle, it has no taste.
Look at it, you cannot see it.
Listen, you cannot hear it.
Use it.

You cannot exhaust it.

➢ The Tao has limitless potential. Much like your leadership, it has no limits. As leaders spend their time gravitating towards the messages of the Tao, there will undoubtedly be moments of agitation, where clarity becomes a challenge and purpose is just a fleeting anomaly. It is in those robust moments where leaders need to sit and be silent in their contemplation. Considering what is known to what is new, that which is present to that which is yet undiscovered. Through these moments of struggle is where illumination finally appears.

#36 – That which will be shrunk
Must first be stretched.
That which will be weakened
Must first be strengthened.
That which will be torn down
Must first be raised up.
That which will be taken
Must first be given.

This is called the "subtle illumination".

The gentle and soft overcomes the hard and
aggressive.

A fish cannot leave the water.

The country's potent weapons
Should not be shown to its people.

➤ Once a leader commits to the purpose of the Tao, s/he begins to see how less, is actually more. Peeling away the layers of what was once a solid understanding of what it takes to lead others slowly gets re-shaped and stretched in a direction where the true purpose becomes self-awareness and self-actualization. These platforms offer leaders a new paradigm for leading and the "subtle illumination" becomes clear over time.

➤ In this journey, do not spend time wallowing in the short-comings that all of us possess. Instead, look to the limitless potential and that which has yet to be revealed to you in your journey. Moving forward in leadership will not be a formula with precise outcomes, but it will eventually display a new vision and pathway for the wholeness that you were designed to be.

#37 – The Tao is always "not doing"
Yet there is nothing it doesn't do.
If the ruler is able to embody it
Everything will naturally change.

Being changed, they desire to act.

So I must restrain them, using the nameless "uncarved
block".

Using the nameless uncarved block
They become desireless.
Desireless, they are tranquil and
All under Heaven is naturally settled.

➤ Purpose and wisdom are the objectives of those who seek the Tao. In leadership, and in life, the choice to adopt this philosophy has consequences. As we live in a microwave society, where results are expected to be seen or achieved in minutes, the life of the Tao is more of a mental and spiritual commitment than it is about tangible results or worldly achievements. To become desireless is to become full or whole, and the sanctity of those moments is where leaders can walk the path of one-ness leading to clarity.

#38 – True virtue is not virtuous
Therefore it has virtue.
Superficial virtue never fails to be virtuous
Therefore it has no virtue.

True virtue does not "act" and has no intentions.
Superficial virtue "acts" and always has intentions.
True humanness "acts" but has no intentions.
True rightness "acts" but has intentions.
True propriety "acts" and if you don't respond
They will roll up their sleeves and threaten you.

Thus, when the Tao is lost there is virtue
When virtue is lost, there is humaneness
When humaneness is lost there is rightness
And when rightness is lost there is propriety.

Now "propriety" is the external appearance of loyalty and
sincerity and the beginning of disorder.
Occult abilities are just flowers of the Tao and the beginning
of foolishness.
Therefore the Master dwells in the substantial and not the
superficial.
Rests in the fruit and not the flower.
So let go of that and grasp this.

➤ The ability to be transparent and respond to the needs of the organization is a principle of leadership. If leaders are only 'acting' the part, there is no authenticity to the gesture. In this light, the 'act' becomes usurped by the true intention. If leaders only respond with tacit language or deeds, they begin to breed a culture of discontent and disorder – both of which will fester in negativity. By dwelling in the substantial and not the superficial, the fruit and not the flower, leaders can release their influence and develop a culture that is wholly balanced and prepared to forge ahead through difficult challenges and uncharted waters.

#39 – These in the past have attained wholeness:
Heaven attains wholeness with its clarity;
The Earth attains wholeness with its firmness;
The Spirit attains wholeness with its transcendence;
The Valley attains wholeness when filled;
The Myriad Things attain wholeness in life;
The Ruler attains wholeness in the correct governance of the people.

In effecting this:
If Heaven lacked clarity it would be divided;
If the Earth lacked firmness it would fly away;
If the Spirit lacked transcendence it would be exhausted;
If the Valley lacked fullness it would be depleted;
If the Myriad Things lacked life they would vanish;
If the Ruler lacks nobility and loftiness he will be tripped up.
Hence
Nobility has lowliness as its root
The High has the Low as its base.

Thus the kings call themselves "the orphan, the lowly, the unworthy".
Is this not taking lowliness as the fundamental? Isn't it?
In this way you can bring about great effect without burden.
Not desiring the rarity of gems or the many-ness of grains of sand.

➢ As the Tao teaches, the sum total of the human experience is to return to the 'uncarved block' through having more by desiring less. That doesn't mean that leaders should sit back and do nothing – but its interpretation is that whatever is chosen to be done, that it be done with an honest favor of humility. IF the challenge is to effect the masses through your leadership influence, the 'great effect' or greater good will be in how the influence shapes decision making, problem solving, setting up the organization, and executing things; big and small, to make the greatest strides within the entity that you serve.

➢ It is through this process that wholeness would be returned to you if the Tao you lead is like "the orphan, the lowly, the unworthy".

#40 – Return is the motion of the Tao.
Softening is its function.
All things in the cosmos arise from being.
Being arises from non-being.

➤ Consider the perceptions that you once had earlier in your career or vocation about leadership; what it should look like, sound like, feel like. What did those images conjure up? Situations or scenarios or feelings or accolades? Because the Tao is limitless and is constant, its purpose is to soften, to provide support, and to relieve us from the limitations that we often place upon ourselves. From this process, our potential can rise from the nothingness that we overlook. There is substantial strength in the leader who can re-invent or re-image themselves toward a new beginning.

#41 – When superior students hear of the Tao
They strive to practice it.
When middling students hear of the Tao
They sometimes keep it and sometimes lose it.
When inferior students hear of the Tao
They have a big laugh.

But "not laughing" in itself is not sufficient to be called the
Tao, and therefore it is said:
The sparkling Tao seems dark
Advancing in the Tao seems like regression.
Settling into the Tao seems rough.

True virtue is like a valley.
The immaculate seems humble.
Extensive virtue seems insufficient.
Established virtue seems deceptive.
The face of reality seems to change.
The great square has no corners.
Great ability takes a long time to perfect.
Great sound is hard to hear.
The great form has no shape.

The Tao is hidden and nameless.
This is exactly why the Tao is good at developing and
perfecting.

➤ In this essay, Lao Tzu is simply reminding all of us dedicated to life and leadership, that the road to enlightenment or illumination is long and difficult. As leaders consider using the Tao as a guide, it may take decades to begin to scratch the surface as to the magnificent comprehension of his reverence or understanding of the Valley, of humility, of the nameless, and the hidden Tao. But he also forces our leadership hand in that our journey of getting it right – getting it almost perfect, is unattainable. Only the Tao is perfect and only the Tao can show us the way. As leaders, it isn't helpful or useful to spend our time beating ourselves up because of our inability to consistently meet the standard each and every time, or hit the bulls eye with one dart. With the Tao as a beacon though, we could spend more time in contemplation and understanding ourselves to build the resilience and courage necessary to approach our 'uncarved block' and practice our individual journey, returning to the innocence from where we came.

#42 – The Tao produces one, one produces two.
The two produce the three and three produce all
things.
All things submit to yin and embrace yang.
They soften their energy to achieve harmony.

People hate to think of themselves as "orphan",
"lowly", and "unworthy".
Yet kings call themselves by these names.

Some lose and yet gain.
Others gain and yet lose.
That which is taught by the people
I also teach:
"The forceful do not choose their place of death".

I regard this as the father of all teachings.

➢ How many times have you been asked to be part of a team because of the skills you bring to the table? As those skills were honed over time, did there become an imbalance in other areas of your leadership? There are moments when we work with others that we will need to soften our energy in order for the team to function at optimal performance. Understanding that one dominating the conversation or the agenda is no longer a leader, but a dictator. And certainly not a member of a highly functioning team.

➢ In ancient times, those kings who regarded themselves with the greatest amount of humility were revered by the masses as the most worthy to learn from. Our organizations could certainly benefit from a landscape of servant leaders more than it could from leaders whose only agenda is self-promotion.

#43 – The softest thing in the world
Will overcome the hardest.
Non-being can enter where there is no space.
Therefore I know the benefit of unattached action.
The wordless teaching, and unattached action.

Are rarely seen.

➢ How many times in your leadership have you been delivered a problem that is clearly not yours, and been expected to solve it for that person? What happens in that moment when you are at the crossroads of enabling vs. empowering? For most people in leadership, avoiding conflict is priority number one. If it is easier to solve the problem ourselves, we do it – sometimes as second nature to how we fashion our leadership style. But if we were to embrace that moment and teach others that the hardest thing isn't the conflict, it's the courage to have the conversation about the issue, we'd likely breed more empowered individuals within our organizations. Leaders can choose to enable or empower at any moment through wordless teaching and unattached action. It only takes courage.

#44 – Which is dearer, fame or your life?
Which is greater, your life or possessions?
Which is more painful, pain or loss?
Therefore we always pay a great price for excessive love
And suffer deep loss for great accumulation.
Knowing what is enough, you will not be humiliated.
Knowing where to stop, you will not be imperiled.

And can be long-standing.

➤ Leaders can be relentless in the drive to climb to the top, but at what cost? If the leader gains by losing, what have they truly achieved? The myriad of things gets in the way of the next rung on the proverbial ladder and is forsaken for the prize at the end. Recognizing this dynamic in your leadership will be critical to your happiness. If you know when 'enough is enough', it is time to change course and re-direct your journey.

#45 – Great perfection seems flawed, yet functions without a hitch.
Great fullness seems empty, yet functions without exhaustion.
Great straightness seems crooked,
Great skill seems clumsy,
Great eloquence seems stammering.

Excitement overcomes cold; stillness overcomes heat.
Clarity and stillness set everything right.

➢ How effective are you when making decisions under duress? Do you ever sense that the pressure of the role you have in the organization is beginning to tax you in ways that you hadn't felt before? Are you capable of making those difficult decisions when time is of the essence? Whether you are a seasoned decision maker or someone who is new to having to make decisions on behalf of others, there is an added weight to your everyday routine.

➢ One of the messages of this essay is the ability to execute informed decisions through the skillful use of clarity and stillness. Regardless of the naysayers, only you, through your leadership, understand the complexity of what you have to endure on any typical day – therefore it is most helpful for you to err on the side of the greater good in order to move your organization forward.

#46 – When the Tao prevails in the land
The horses leisurely graze and fertilize the ground.
When the Tao is lacking in the land
War-horses are bred outside the city.
Natural disasters are not as bad as not knowing what
is enough.
Loss is not as bad as wanting more.

Therefore the sufficiency that comes from knowing
what is enough is an eternal sufficiency.

> If the Tao that you follow is filled with angst and desire, you will surely fall short of your aspirations. However, when the Tao you follow sufficiently rests in goodness, fruit can be harvested from your trees.

> If you consider your leadership space as a land that has to be cultivated, you are then responsible for everything that happens. How is the soil nourished? Are you selecting the right plants to be grown? Will you have the energy and resilience to work through those crops that fail with the same resilience as those that are successful? All of this for the leader has to be considered. And when the season ends, will you have a greater appreciation for sufficiency? Will you understand to a broader extent what it takes to perform your role with a new potential? All of this must be taken into consideration if you intend to grow as a leader.

#47 – Without going out the door, knowing
everything,
Without peaking out the window shades, seeing the
Way of Heaven.

The further you go, the less you know.

The sage understands without having to go through
the whole process.

She is famous without showing herself.

Is perfected without striving.

➤ The path of leadership, wisdom, and purpose is complex. It will offer many challenging opportunities, providing a platform for evolution in yourself, and those around you. In what ways are you adopting a holistic approach to your leadership?

➤ Do you see leadership as black/white, right/wrong, this/that? By remaining exclusive in your options, you limit the potential that exists in yourself and in others. Consider what it might be like to be on the receiving end of a two-sided choice – on one side you feel listened to or validated, yet on the other, the exact opposite. If you open yourself to being able to peek through the windowshade just long enough to see other options, you may very well walk away from your obligations with a greater sense of self and a more complete leader.

#48 – In studying, each day is gained.
In following the Tao, each day something is lost.
Lost and again lost.
Until there is nothing left to do.
Not-doing, nothing is left undone.
You can possess the world by never manipulating it.
No matter how much you manipulate.
You can never possess the world.

➢ This is the mystery of the Tao – to work without recognition, and to gain each day, by losing. The most selfless among us who adopts that Tao is constantly seeking the unknown, in order to discover a greater layer of work and understanding of themselves. There is no mystery to the intent – but there is always mystery in what might be discovered. If you possess the courage to adopt the Tao, then you must be patient to accept the loss in yourself, as well as when the enlightened moment appears. Contemplate the unknown and be still – do not massage it for your own satisfaction. Manipulating it will only cause a false sense of self and angst. Be honest, be truthful, be authentic with yourself first – then, when that moment of clarity reveals itself, you will be ready for the next phase of work in your development.

#49 – The sage has no fixed mind,
She takes the mind of the people as her mind.

I treat the good as good; I also treat the evil as good.
This is true goodness.
I trust the trustworthy; I also trust the untrustworthy.
This is real trust.

When the sage lives with people, she harmonizes with
them.
And conceals her mind for them.
The sages treat them as their little children.

➤ It isn't uncommon to have people in your circle that you go to when you are in need. You trust them for the myriad of things that they possess. But, when was the most recent time that you placed your trust in someone other than those in your circle? Can you identify those who you'd like to have a better relationship with, but they do not share that same desire? If this is you, start small, and let go of the pressure that keeps you tethered to that untrusting dynamic. Instead of asking yourself, 'what will happen to me if they don't come through?'; ask yourself, 'what might we achieve with their support and capacity for a new tomorrow if they do?' At the end of the day, you can demonstrate a higher level of reliance and trust within yourself.

#50 – Coming into life and entering death,
The followers of life are three in ten.
The followers of death are three in ten.
Those whose life activity is their death ground are
three in ten.
Why is this?
Because they live life grasping for its rich taste.

Now I have heard that those who are expert in
handling life.
Can travel the land without meeting tigers and rhinos,
Can enter battle without being wounded.
The rhino has no place to plant its horn,
The tiger has no place to place its claws,
Weapons find no place to receive their sharp edges.
Why?

Because he has no death-ground.

➢ There is a difference between being fearless and fearful of your own leadership. But there is great solace in knowing thyself and having the strength to forge through the difficult times with a fearless abandon.

➢ If the leader behaves like the rhino or the tiger it will die on the hill that is climbed. Because the weapons are claws and horn, there is armor to fight with, and sharp edges to defend. Without these weapons, leaders have their minds. And that is perhaps the strongest weapon to defend against.

#51 – Tao gives birth to it,
Virtue rears it,
Materiality shapes it,
Activity perfects it.

Therefore, there are none of the myriad things who
do not venerate the Tao or esteem its virtue.
This veneration of the Tao and esteeming of its virtue
is something they do naturally, without being forced.
Therefore, Tao gives birth.

Its virtue rears, develops, raises, adjusts, and
disciplines, nourishes, covers, and protects, produces
but does not possess, acts without expectation, and
leads without forcing.

This is called "Mysterious Virtue".

➤ Choose but one of these to embrace over time – rearing, developing, raising, adjusting, self-discipline, nourishing, covering, protecting, acting without expectation, and leading without forcing. After a period of time, reflect in your stillness and nothingness. Your leadership wisdom and purpose will shine anew and the Tao will be honored from your effort.

➤ The Mysterious Virtue is unattainable without effort and unrealized without commitment.

➤ Illumination is impossible without an appetite to know more. Knowing more results in knowledge that is simple, which is the intent of the Tao.

#52 – All things have a beginning, which we can regard
as their Mother.
Knowing the mother, we can know its children.
Knowing the children, yet still cleaving to the mother
You can die without pain.

Stop up the holes
Shut the doors,
You can finish your life without anxiety.

Open the doors,
Increase your involvements,
In the end you can't be helped.

Seeing the subtle is called illumination.
Keeping flexible is called strength.
Use the illumination, but return to the light.
Don't bring harm to yourself.

This is called "practicing the eternal".

➢ There is great strength in demonstrating flexibility for leaders who have the courage to exercise it. The goal for the ego-driven leader is to be perceived as almighty. For leaders embracing the Tao, the light is the driving force – therefore there is no consideration of the 'what ifs'. If your leadership is steeped in goodness toward the cause, as well as the people that are helping to achieve that end, it isn't helpful to spend any time in negativity once the mind is clear of anxiety. Flexibility releases the ego and chaos.

#53 – If I had just a little bit of wisdom
I should walk the Great Path and fear only straying
from it.
Though the Way is quite broad
People love shortcuts.

The court is immaculate,
While the fields are overgrown with weeds,
And the granaries are empty.
They wear silk finery,
Carry sharp swords,
Sate themselves on food and drink
Having wealth in excess.
They are called thieving braggarts.

This is definitely not the Way.

➤ While it is true that there are no shortcuts in life, the same holds true for leadership. What many leaders fail to realize in their journey is that as quickly as they arrived at their perceptions of success, they can just as quickly fall. There are many circumstances that can cause that decent; money, notoriety, arrogance, leading a life of excess – each or one of these has the ability to take everything away that you have worked so hard to achieve. This is not the intention of the Tao.

➤ By being mindful of your words and actions, you can have a greater perspective on how you spend your time, who you spend it with, and where you choose to spend it. Make those choices carefully.

#54 – The well established cannot be uprooted.
The well-grasped does not slip away.
Generation after generation carries out the ancestor.
Worship without break.

Cultivate it in yourself and virtue will be real.
Cultivate it in the family and virtue will overflow.
Cultivate it in the town and virtue will be great.
Cultivate it in the country and virtue will be abundant.
Cultivate it in the world and virtue will be everywhere.

Therefore, take yourself and observe yourself.
Take the family and observe the family.
Take the town and observe the town.
Take the country and observe the country.
Take the world and observe the world.

How do I know the world as it is?

By this.

➤ There is a certain level of honesty that every good leader possesses when it comes to reflecting on their performance. Some days are solid, while others can be a struggle to find one morsel of satisfaction in the day. This is part of the landscape of leadership.

➤ If the leader looks to the outside world and then inward for inspiration, motivation, or even confidence, the standard will most always be worldly in its intent. This process is far too complex to sustain. Instead, look from the inside-out; start with yourself, then look to the other layers of the world in which you work, live, and play.

➤ By looking inward, an honest assessment of where you are and where you are going in leadership can be adapted to the world around you, instead of the other way around. Looking inward, then outward, you can set your own standard based on the needs that are revealed to you. Start small, then evolve to greater spaces.

#55 – One who remains rich in virtuous power
is like a newborn baby.
Bees, scorpions, and venomous snakes do not bite it,
The wild beasts do not attack it,
Birds of prey do not sink their claws into it.
Though its bones are weak
And muscles soft
Its grip is strong.
Without knowing of the blending of male and female
S/he is a perfect production;
The ultimate vitality.
S/he cries all day without getting hoarse.
S/he is the ultimate harmony.

Understanding harmony is called the Constant.
Knowing the Constant is called illumination.
Nourishing life is called blessing.
Having control of your breath is called strength.

After things blossom they decay, and
This is called the non-Tao.

The non-Tao expires quickly.

➤ As the Tao evolves in the lives of leaders, there
   will be moments of great illumination through a
   reflective calmness of understanding the greater
   awareness of just who you are.

➤ As this process unfolds, leaders discover the
   Constant, or harmony, in their role, and
   eventually gravitate towards that end.

➤ Through this process, the nourishment of life is
   presented, and leaders feel a sense of fulfillment
   not in their achievements, but in the way they
   have begun to shape the world around them.

➤ In these moments when illumination is present,
   and harmony is the Constant, and blessings
   abound, this is when strength emerges due to an
   understanding of vast potential.

#56 – One who knows does not speak.
One who speaks, does not know.
Close your holes, shut your doors,
Soften your sharpness, loosen your knots.
Soften your glare and merge with the everyday.

This is called mysteriously attaining oneness.

Though you cannot possess it, you are intimate with it
And at the same time; distant.
Though you cannot possess it, you are benefitted by
it, and harmed by it.
You cannot possess it, but are esteemed through it
And humbled by it.

Therefore the world values you.

➤ Seeking oneness with your world as a leader requires that individuals exercise an uncommon degree of patience with themselves. When the leader feels compelled to speak, s/he listens. When s/he has been offended, there is no striking back, but instead, calmness. When the pressures of the day seem too much to handle, there is serenity. This is what it means to practice oneness with your surroundings.

➤ As oneness is not a possession, it can only be achieved when leaders are willing to trust the process and walk alongside it, being a passenger to its journey, and a companion to its mission.

#57 – Use fairness in governing the state.
Use surprise tactics in war.

Be unconcerned and you will have the world.
How do I know this?
Because:
The more regulations there are,
The poorer people become.
The more people own lethal weapons,
The more darkened are the country and clans.
The more clever the people are,
The more extraordinary actions they take,
The more picky the laws are,
The more thieves and gangsters there are.

Therefore, the sages say:

I do not force my way and the people transform
themselves.
I enjoy my serenity and the people correct themselves.
I do not interfere and the people enrich themselves.
I have no desires. And the people find their original
mind.

➢ Leaders are capable, through their wisdom and purpose to cultivate a team of people to perform important work. When that happens, the leader must back away from the team long enough to allow them to perform their work. Micro-managing all the time will only cause decay.

➢ When members of the team or the organization demonstrate their competence, the leader recognizes them for their offering(s) and demonstrates a degree of serenity, which in turn is reflected upon the people.

➢ If leaders 'mingle' too much, the work can never get done. Do not sabotage the work before it is even born.

#58 – When the government is laid-back
The people are relaxed.
When the government is nitpicking
The people have anxiety.
Misfortune depends upon fortune.
Fortune conceals misfortune.
What has a definite delimitation?
Or abnormality?

The normal reverts to strangeness.
Goodness reverts to perversion.

People certainly have been confused for a long time.

Therefore the sage squares things without cutting;
Edges without separating.
Straightens without lining up.

Shines but does not glare.

➢ Creating a synergistic culture in the workplace is a talent that many leaders struggle to find. If the leader is too difficult to work with, there is separation. If the leader is too easy, the perception is that they don't care. Striking this balance takes time and talent, but most importantly, it takes a highly effective communicator. A leader who can bring together many people toward a common goal, allow flexibility to align with being accountable, and one who can illuminate but not outshine, stands to have a long career in leadership.

#59 – In governing the country and serving Heaven
There is nothing like frugality.
Only by being frugal can you recover quickly.
When you recover quickly you accumulate virtue.
Having accumulated virtue,
There is nothing you can't overcome.
When there is nothing you can't overcome
Who knows the limits of your capabilities?
These limits being unfathomable
You can possess the country.

The Mother who possesses the country can be long-living.
This is called "planting the roots deeply and firmly".

The way to a long life and eternal vision.

➢ How often have leaders, due to an excessive disposition, fallen in their journey? Because there is nothing like frugality, if some of it is lost, it wasn't much to begin with, so it recovers quickly. Through experience and time, accumulating virtue along the way, the leader begins to reach their purpose or potential. And when this unfolds, there is limitless potential to what can be accomplished. Doing this in all areas of life offers similar rewards.

#60 – Ruling a large country is like cooking a small fish.
When you govern people with the Tao
Demons will have no power.
Not that they don't have power,
But their power will not harm people.

Since the sage doesn't harm people,
The two will not harm each other.

Here their power merges and returns.

➢ In this essay Lao Tzu infers that leadership can be like cooking a small fish. If it is handled too roughly, it can be damaged. The same is true of the people that you lead. Leaders that are dedicated to following the Tao are mindful of the way that they treat people. They look to offer support, and do not look to damage the individual. Because the Tao is inclusive of a disposition that is welcoming, demons to do their work.

#61 –The great state should be like a river basin.
The mixing place of the world;
The feminine of the world.
The feminine always overcomes the masculine by
softness, because softness is lesser.
Therefore if a large state serves a small state
It will gain the small state.
If a small state serves a large state
It will gain the large state.

Therefore some serve in order to gain
And some gain despite their servitude.

The large state wants nothing more
Than to unite and feed its people.
The small state wants nothing more
Than to enter into the service of the right person.
Thus, both get what they want.

Greatness lies in placing oneself below.

➤ According to the messages of the Tao, to lead is to serve. Whether you are in a small organization or a large one, approaching leadership from a service-oriented disposition is a choice.

➤ In the process of adopting a servitude philosophy, understand that your altruistic attitude should not supplant accountability – both of yourself, and for others. In difficult moments when holding people accountable, you can exercise servitude by offering support, training, or guidance in a helpful and respectful manner. Greatness in leading offers all of these useful interventions, but does not dismiss the accountability needed to move your organization forward.

#62 – The Tao is hidden deeply in all things.
It is the treasure of the good
And the refuge of the not-so-good.
With skillful words you can be successful.
With honorable actions you can be included.

People may not be so good, but how can you deny
them?

Therefore, even though there are great jewels
brought in by teams of horses at the coronation of
the emperor and the installation of the three princes,
This is not as good as staying where you are
And advancing in the Tao.

Why did ancients so value the Tao?

You can't say that it was for seeking gain
Or to have punishments to deter crime.

Therefore it is the most prized in the world.

➢ Seeking wisdom and purpose through the Tao offers its followers many paths. While the Tao is rooted in its intent, there will be moments in your leadership where you are tested. In those testing moments, while they may enticing, Lao Tzu suggests that you not follow the path well traveled, instead, stay dedicated and committed to where you would like to go, and who you strive to become. Do not be fooled by people or moments which pull you away from your maximum potential for the sake of fame or fortune – by staying true to yourself, your roots will continue to grow firmly.

#63 – Do without "doing".
Get involved without manipulating.
Taste without tasting.
Make the great small,
The many, few.
Respond to anger with virtue.
Deal with difficulties while they are still easy.
Handle the great while it is still small.

The difficult problems in life
Always start off being simple.
Great affairs always start off being small.
Therefore the sage never deals with the great
And is able to actualize his greatness.

Now light words generate little belief,
Much ease turns into much difficulty.
Therefore the sage treats things as though they were
difficult,
And hence, never has difficulty.

➢ There are many lessons in this essay that speak to the challenges and journey to improved leadership. "The difficult problems in life always start off being simple." Very true – however, as most people are uncomfortable with handling or embracing conflict, those problems might get more complex, and in the end be more difficult to overcome.

➢ If you are willing to invite the process of working through conflict into your leadership or personal life, and are steadfast in handling the small problems, along with the large ones with a host of leadership competencies, you will have fewer problems to work through.

#64 – That which is at rest is easy to grasp.
That which has not yet come about is easy to plan for.
That which is fragile is easily broken.
That which is minute is easily scattered.
Handle things before they arise.
Manage affairs before they are in a mess.

A thick tree grows from a tiny seed.
A tall building arises from a mound of earth.
A journey of a thousand miles begins with one step.
Contriving, you are defeated;
Grasping, you lose.

The sage doesn't contrive, so she isn't beaten.
Not grasping, she doesn't lose.
When people are carrying out their projects
They usually blow it at the end.
If you are as careful at the end as you were in the beginning,
you won't be disappointed.
Therefore the sage desires non-desire,
Does not value rare goods,
Studies the un-learnable
So that she can correct the mistakes of average people
And aid in all things manifesting their true nature.

Without presuming to take the initiative.

➢ If nascent leaders are able to anchor their leadership philosophy in the Tao, the path toward illumination becomes fully realized. If there is a weak foundation in words and actions for the leader, they are sure to fall. By prioritizing the many details of the day in the life of a leader, the leader is better able to move and progress through their day/week/month with a more comprehensive understanding. Ignoring the difficult or spending time avoiding the challenges only makes them worse.

➢ By freeing yourself of the noise that comes with leading others, your journey can be fulfilled. Carrying out the projects of the day and attending to them with the same degree of attention to detail, energy, enthusiasm, and spirit will offer a renewed sense of potential for yourself, and for those you lead.

#65 – The ancients who were skillful at the Tao
Did not illuminate the people
But rather kept them simple.
When the people are difficult to rule
It is because of their cleverness.

Therefore, if you use cleverness to rule the state
You are a robber of the state.
If you don't use cleverness to rule the state
You are a blessing to the state.

If you understand these two points, you know the
proper norm for governing.
To be continuously understanding the proper norm is
called Mysterious Virtue.
How deep and far-reaching Mysterious Virtue is!
It makes all return.

Until they reach the Great Norm.

➢ Honesty, authenticity, candor; these will be helpful to you in your leadership life. The opposite; dishonesty, undermining, or scapegoating, will turn away those that report to you. By creating a culture of trust amongst the people, things can get done the way they were intended to. In your capacity to lead, choose those attributes that will build your integrity and bring out the most in others so that they might be able to see the greatness within themselves.

#66 ~ The reason the river and sea can be regarded
as the rulers of all the valley streams
Is because of their being below them.
Therefore they can be their rulers.
So if you want to be over people
You must speak humbly to them.
If you want to lead them
You must place yourself behind them.

Thus the sage is positioned above
And the people do not feel oppressed.
He is in front and they feel nothing wrong.
Therefore they like to push him front and never
resent him.

Since he does not contend

No one can contend with him.

➢ If the true capacity of a leader following the Tao is measured by their ability to lead from behind, the success of the leader to execute this task is in the ability to let go and be humble. It isn't uncommon for leaders to have complete control over various phases of their world – and in some cases, it is better that way. However, as the team or group of people evolve, so too should the leader in their ability to allow the people to do the work. In those moments, the leader becomes the guide-on-the-side, supporting the mission and the people as one entity.

#67 – The reason that everyone calls my Tao great is because there is nothing quite like it.
It is exactly because it is great that there is nothing quite like it. If there were something that were consistently like it, how could it be small?

I have three treasures that I hold and cherish. The first is compassion. The second is frugality. The third is not daring to put myself ahead of everybody.

Having compassion, I can be brave.
Having frugality, I can be generous.
Not daring to put myself ahead of everybody I can take the time to perfect my abilities.
Now if I am brave without compassion
Generous without frugality, or
Go to the fore without putting my own concerns last, I might as well be dead.

If you wage war with compassion you will win.
If you protect yourself with compassion you will be impervious.

Heaven will take care of you, protecting you with compassion.

➤ The leadership challenge: Each day, select an attribute that you believe is going to help you become a better leader. It could be compassion, patience, honesty, frugality, selflessness, grace, humility, or solace. Allow everything that you do in that day to be reflective of or radiate that attribute – from the way that you go about holding meetings with your team to the interactions that you have with others outside of your circle. Try that for a month – then go back to your self-reflections and ask if you are a more effective leader. You will be surprised at your re-birth!

#68 – The best warrior is never aggressive.
The best fighter is never angry.
The best tactician does not engage with enemy.
The best utilizer of people's talents places himself
below them.

This is called the virtue of non-contention.
It is called the ability to engage people's talents.
It is called the ultimate in merging with Heaven.

➤ The Tao encourages leaders to offer themselves as an example of illumination. Working through the Mysterious Virtue and understanding the purpose of the message allows leaders to broaden their respective options in working with others. If you as a leader are aggressive, angry, or negatively intentional with others, you move away from the Tao.

➤ To find a place and a purpose for someone's talents to be revealed is to honor the role of leader that you have been given. Putting the 'right people on the bus, and in the right seats' is part of your challenge. Work until the bus can be driven by the people, so that you can take a seat in the back.

#69 – Strategists have a saying;
I prefer to be able to move, rather than being in a
fixed position
I prefer to retreat a foot rather than advancing an
inch.
This is called progress without advancing;
Preparing without showing off;
Smashing where there is no defense;
Taking him without a fight.

There is no greater danger than under-estimating
your opponent.
If I underestimate my opponent I will lose that which is
most dear.

Therefore, when opponents clash, the one who is
sorry about it will be the winner.

➤ While it is hopeful that your leadership will be the vehicle that gets your organization to maximize its potential, it is rarely achieved without moments of struggle with outside forces. Some of those things can be predictable, while others may be unforeseen. This is why it is important to plan for the known and the unknown; to be poised to weather the storm, and get beyond circumstances which might cripple another organization.

➤ Of the many dangers in underestimating your opponents, remember that evolving is the key. Do not be left behind because of the foolhardy position of 'that's the way we've always done it' or through a lack of technological savvy. As a leader it is up to you to look for the dangers that are ahead.

#70 – My words are easy to understand
And easy to practice.
Yet nobody understands them or practices them.
My words have an origin;
My actions have a principle.
It is only because of your not understanding this
That you do not understand me.
Since there are few who understand me
I am valued.
Therefore the sage wears coarse clothes.
Yet hides a jewel in his bosom.

➢ One of the objectives of the Tao is to seek understanding. By moving along in the journey, the once unexplained becomes explainable, the unknowing is learned, and the unreachable becomes attainable. If those principles can be followed in the Tao, so too can they be applied to leadership. Seek greater understanding of the challenges and the people around you. Strive to end discord amongst groups and listen to their world, before you offer them a piece of your own. To be understood, is to understand.

#71 – There is nothing better than to know that you don't know.
Not knowing, yet thinking you know – this is sickness.

Only when you are sick of being sick, can you be cured.
The sage's not being sick
Is because she is sick of sickness.

Therefore she is not sick.

➢ Leaders endure much through the course of their day – hopefully, much of that is productive. Yet there are times when tolerance and patience get tested. In those moments, and in the leadership journey with the Tao, cling to what you know, and understand what you don't know. If you try and fake it, you will be seen as untrustworthy. If this pattern repeats itself time and again, you will become, as Lao Tzu states, sick. What he means is that you cannot expect different results by doing the same things. You have to change things up and be tired of feeling whatever emotion you feel inside you that is holding you back from progressing. The definition of insanity is just that – doing the same thing over and over and thinking that you'll get a different result. Once you are sick and tired of being sick and tired you will advance yourself toward a new path, and different results.

#72 – When the people do not fear your might
Then your might has truly become great.
Don't interfere with their household affairs.
Don't depress their livelihood.

If you don't oppress them they won't feel oppressed.

Thus the sage understands herself
But does not show herself.
Loves herself
But does not prize herself.
Therefore she lets go of that

And takes this.

➤ Pride goeth before the fall. This statement from biblical times rings true for leaders today. If you are in leadership because you enjoy the power more than you appreciate the influence, your career will be cut short. If you oppress others, that may be the sword that you die on in the end. If you desire to become great at leading, become small, allow yourself to be understood, and seek only the goodness in others. Be mindful that you will be disappointed along the way – but that disappointment is not yours to own, it belongs to the one who is not on the same journey with the Tao.

#73 – If you are courageous in daring you will die.
If you are courageous in not-daring you will live.
Among these two, one is beautiful and the other is
harmful.

Who understands the reason why Heaven dislikes
what it dislikes?
Even the sage has difficulty in knowing this.

The Way of Heaven is to win easily without struggle.

To respond well without words,
To naturally come without special invitation,
To plan well without anxiety.

Heaven's net is vast
It is loose.

Yet nothing slips through.

➢ This essay is one that is extremely complex. And certainly for leaders, their days are filled with complexities that most people might not be able to withstand. Being courageous in leadership asks individuals to take measured risks to enhance the position of their organization. If the risk is too big, so too could be the negative results. However, being courageous in your words, and actions, and responding to those who need you in a timely manner offers them a safety net. If your net is vast, it will embrace all within it in an inclusive manner. The best leaders make certain that nobody falls through. The challenge before you is to determine how wide of a net you desire to cast.

#74 – If the people don't fear death
How will you scare them with death?
If you make the people continuously fear death
By seizing anybody who does something out of the
ordinary
And killing them,
Who will dare to move?

There is always an official executioner to handle this.
If you play the role of the official executioner
It is like cutting wood in the capacity of Master
Carpenter.

There will be few who will not cut their hands.

➤ What is your threshold for creativity amongst
your team? Do you allow for individuals to set
the standard for ideas to be offered for
consideration? Some of the most successful
leaders discovered in their own journey that once
this element was present in their workplace, the
culture began to change for the better. If you as
the leader are seen by co-workers to be the killer
of ideas and creativity, you eventually will foster a
group of robots – doing the minimum and never
reaching their potential. If you can embrace the
Tao's aim to teach others that there is a degree
of latitude in their work, the work will be refined,
and so too will the person.

#75 – The reason people starve
Is because their rulers tax them excessively.
They are difficult to govern because their rulers have
their own ends in mind.

The reason people take death lightly
Is because they want life to be rich.
Therefore they take death lightly.
It is only by not living for your own ends
That you can go beyond valuing life.

➤ Is your team working overtime for a quota to be met? Have you raised the bar so high that it becomes an unattainable and reasonable goal? When this occurs in the workplace, dissention begins to grow, and energy is sapped from the team. At that point, the team becomes difficult to lead. Constantly pushing ahead without appreciation or to satisfy your own agenda is the complete opposite of the Tao. This becomes the birthplace of indignance.

#76 – When people are born they are gentle and soft.
At death they are hard and stiff.
When plants are alive they are soft and delicate.
When they die, they wither and dry up.
Therefore the hard and stiff are followers of death.
The gentle and soft are the followers of life.

Thus if you are aggressive and stiff, you won't win.
When a tree is hard enough, it is cut.

Therefore the hard and big are lesser,
The gentle and soft are greater.

➢ It isn't likely that leaders desire to be associated with the words 'soft' or 'gentle', but in following the Tao, the lesson is that it is the greatest of those who display these attributes that are the closest to reaching their potential.

➢ In arguing, be honest with your opponent, be firm, but be gentle in the words that you choose to convey your message. If the message is arranged in that fashion, the groundwork has been laid for future conversations to take place. Seek the win-win, but be honest with yourself and those around you that the outcome will not always work in that favor.

#77 – The Way of Heaven
Is like stretching a bow.
The top is pulled down,
The bottom is pulled up
Excess string is removed
Where more is needed, it is added.

It is the Way of Heaven
To remove where there is excess
And add where there is lack.
The way of people is different:
They take away where there is need
And add where there is surplus.

Who can take his surplus and give it to the people?
Only one who possesses the Tao.

Therefore the sage acts without expectation.
Does not abide in his accomplishments.
Does not want to show his virtue.

➤ When leaders begin to share their knowledge, time, skill, understanding with others, the net that they cast becomes larger. If you as the leader see a need in the people that you serve, fulfill it. If there is a way that you can connect with them, embrace that opportunity to show them who you are, what you value, and what they should expect from you. Examine where there is surplus in your organization - not in goods and services, but in people and processes - offer consideration that the surplus could be useful in other ways. In creating a balance for your people, they will learn that part of your vision is grounded with equity.

#78 – Nothing in the world is softer than water,
Yet nothing is better at overcoming the hard and
strong.
This is because nothing can alter it.

That the soft overcomes the hard
And the gentle overcomes the aggressive
Is something that everybody knows,
But none can do themselves.

Therefore the sages say:

The one who accepts the dirt of the state;
Becomes its master.
The one who accepts its calamity;
Becomes king of the world.

Truth seems contradictory.

➤ Taking the good with the bad in leadership and in life is just part of the process. There will be moments of great happiness, and moments of profound sorrow. Building your resilience toward accepting this as part of the daily routine in leadership is quite simply the way it is. However, when those exciting moments take place, be reminded of the purpose of the Tao – and when those difficult moments arise, be gentle and soft.

#79 – After calming great anger
There are always resentments left over.
How can this be considered as goodness?
Therefore the sage keeps her part of the deal
And doesn't check-up on the other person.

Thus virtuous officials keep their promise
And the crooked ones break it.

The Heavenly Tao has no favorites.

It raises up the Good.

➢ If you cannot build trust as a leader, you cannot build a team to reach their potential. Period.

#80 – Let there be a small country with few people,
Who, even having much machinery, don't use it.
Who take death seriously and don't wander far away.
Even though they have boats and carriages, they
never ride in them.
Having armor and weapons, they never go to war.
Let them return to measurement by tying knots in
rope.

Sweeten their food, give them nice clothes, a peaceful
abode and a relaxed life.

Even though the next country can be seen and its
dogs and chickens can be heard,
The people will grow old and die without visiting each
other's land.

➤ How much excess do you need in your leadership life to satiate your desires? Will 'more' of anything quench your appetite, or will you remain hungry for the next acquisition? In the end, what will you have accumulated? How much 'enough' is enough? This disposition is not the way of the Tao. Additionally, if the leader who has everything doesn't have the understanding that there are people and communities who are lacking, how will that leader ever truly learn the lesson of perspective?

#81 – True words are not fancy.
Fancy words are not true.
The good do not debate.
Debaters are not good.
The one who really knows is not broadly learned,
The extensively learned do not really know.
The sage does not hoard,
She gives people her surplus.
Giving her surplus to others she is enriched.

The way of Heaven is to help and not harm.

➢ The way of Heaven is to help and not harm.
➢ The way of Heaven is to help and not harm.
➢ The way of Heaven is to help and not harm.
➢ The way of Heaven is to help and not harm.
➢ The way of Heaven is to help and not harm.
➢ The way of Heaven is to help and not harm.
➢ The way of Heaven is to help and not harm.
➢ The way of Heaven is to help and not harm.
➢ The way of Heaven is to help and not harm.
➢ The way of Heaven is to help and not harm.
➢ The way of Heaven is to help and not harm.
➢ The way of Heaven is to help and not harm.
➢ The way of Heaven is to help and not harm.
➢ The way of Heaven is to help and not harm.

This is the true meaning of the Tao

Bibliography

Each of the essays were taken from the translations and notes by Yi-Ping Ong and Charlie Muller with George Stade as Consulting Editorial Director, Barnes & Noble Classics, New York, New York, 2005.

57960680R00093

Made in the USA
San Bernardino, CA
23 November 2017